A Christmas Wish, a title in the Tiny Tea series

© 2001 by Dee Appel
Published by Blue Cottage Gifts™, a division of Multnomah Publishers, Inc.
P.O. Box 1720, Sisters, OR 97759

ISBN 1-58860-029-7

Artwork by Gay Talbott Boassy
All works of art reproduced in this book are copyrighted by Gay Talbott Boassy and may not be reproduced without the artist's permission. For more information regarding art featured in this book, please contact:

> Mr. Gifford B. Bowne II
> Indigo Gate, Inc.
> 1 Pegasus Drive
> Colts Neck, NJ 07722
> (732) 577-9333

Designed by Koechel Peterson & Associates, Minneapolis, Minnesota

Scripture quotation taken from *The Holy Bible*, New International Version (NIV) © 1973, 1984 by International Bible Society, used by permission of Zondervan Publishing House.

Printed in China

01 02 03 04 05 06 — 10 9 8 7 6 5 4 3 2 1 0

www.bluecottagegifts.com

A Christmas Wish

TEXT BY **DEE APPEL**   ART BY **GAY TALBOTT BOASSY**

BLUE COTTAGE GIFTS™

a division of Multnomah Publishers, Inc.
Sisters, Oregon

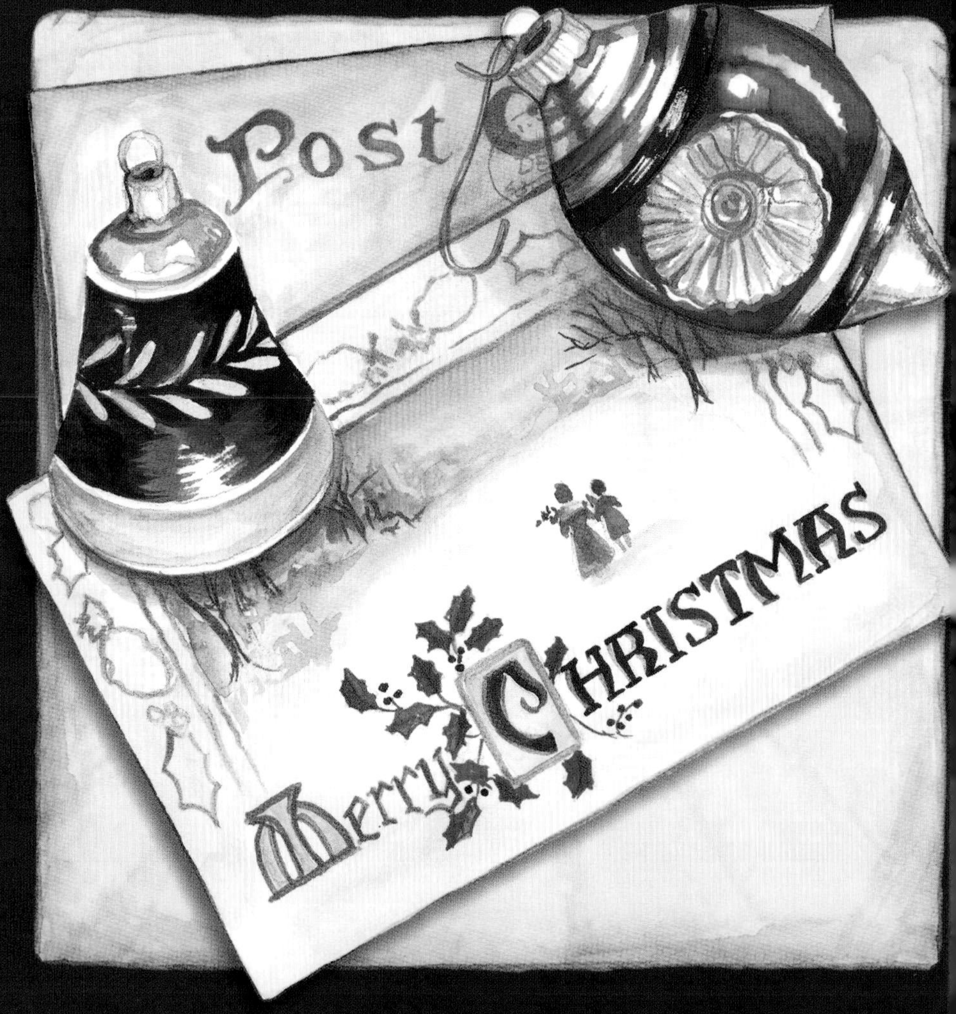
Post
Merry CHRISTMAS

'Tis the season of good cheer
When old friends come
from far and near,

When sweet, sweet fragrance
fills the air,
And hearts o'erflow
with love to share.

Mem'ries rush

of days gone by

And flush with joy

of days yet nigh.

The air is crisp
and bright with lights
That twink and sparkle
through the night.

Amidst the bustle and the rush,
Seize a moment
when things are hushed,

*And brew a Christmas
Tiny Tea,
Pause a moment
and think of me.*

I wish you well,
my Dear Olde Friend,
And think of you
as this year ends,

$\mathcal{R}$ecalling days
now long gone by
$\mathcal{W}$hen we were younger,
you and $\mathcal{I}$...

So when you briefly
stop to sup
The Christmas tea
that fills your cup,

*Feel the warmth
as this year ends,
And steep yourself
in the love of friends.*

This is The **CHRISTMAS** STORY

Merry

LUKE 2: 8-11

And The Good News For ALL Who TRUST iN JESUS

I have not stopped
giving thanks for you,
remembering you in my prayers.

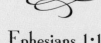

Ephesians 1:16

LOVE IN CHRIST

DELORES
CORLEY